# A Day in the Life
# of An Adult with ADHD
## (Attention Deficit/Hyperactivity Disorder)

Vera Joffe, Ph.D.
and
Monica Iachan, B.A.

Foreword by Russell Barkley, Ph.D.
Illustrated by Margaret Scott
1st Edition in the United States

Library of Congress Control Number: 2006935412
Requests for books should contact:
www.verajoffe.com
(954)-341-4441

# Dedication

I would like to dedicate this book to my parents, Isaac and Thea Joffe, and to my wonderful daughters, Melissa and Monica Iachan. Let the values that I received from my parents continue to go from one generation to another: the importance of family, affection, studies, justice, and consideration for others. To Melissa and Monica for reminding me of the most important role in my life: of being the mother and friend to these two young women who have their own ideas, opinions, dreams, careers, and roles in society.

This book is also dedicated to Margaret Scott's mother, Doris, in loving memory.

# Foreword

Nearly all books on adults with ADHD written for them describe the characteristics of the disorder (the symptoms) and rattle off a list of the likely impairments those adults may experience. This is fine as a starting point. After all, that is how the disorder is actually diagnosed – by using a list of symptoms for the disorder and determining how many a person may be experiencing, when they developed, and whether or not they are interfering with the person's functioning in any major life activities. Such approaches are based on descriptions of the disorder and the people who have it. But that is not a theory of the disorder – a conceptual understanding of what is actually going astray in a person's psychological development who may have ADHD and why it is leading them to behave the way that they do.

After a century of research that describes the characteristics of people with ADHD, we have only recently moved into building theories about ADHD. The beauty of this book is that it is based on these new views of ADHD founded in a theory of ADHD, not merely on a description of its surface features. Theories try to answer the great "why" questions we may have about ADHD – why do the symptoms develop as they do, present in the way they do, lead to the kinds of impairments they are likely to produce. In short, they tell us just what is going wrong in ADHD. And by doing that a good theory gives us not only a greater insight into the disorder, but also into how best to treat it. That is what you will discover in this book – a new way of looking at ADHD that gives greater insight into this disorder and into how one might better manage it.

As Dr. Joffe nicely explains here, viewing ADHD as a disorder of attention or of excessive activity level is comparable to viewing autism as just hand flapping, being socially aloof, and talking oddly. Both are rather superficial views of a disorder. For as it turns out, the attention problems we see in ADHD are not really problems with attention specifically but arise from a more profound problem in the development of the brain's executive system and so of the self-control that system provides to humans. The executive system allows us to plan, organize, and direct behavior toward the future because it permits us to hold multiple events in our minds and so bind them together that would otherwise be separated in time. This tells us that the person with ADHD is not inattentive to their surroundings in the moment – to the contrary they are often too attentive to such things. They are inattentive to the future, to the things they should be thinking about, holding in mind, preparing or planning for, organizing toward, and accomplishing so as to get ready for future events. They are, in a real sense, inattentive to time. That is a profound disturbance and it is one of the central messages of this book.

Just as important to understand is that the hyperactivity often seen in the disorder is itself a manifestation of a problem with inhibition or impulsiveness. And that problem is linked to the difficulties with executive abilities and self-control because those abilities and self-control are dependent on one's ability to stop, inhibit, and wait. The executive faculties cannot guide behavior toward the future if one is always responding on impulse to the moment. Truly, everything comes to those who can wait – everything in this case is everything one needs to be thinking about and getting ready for that lie ahead in time. Both of these theoretical shifts provide a relatively radical change in how one views or understands and hence manages the disorder.

Out of this theoretical understanding of ADHD comes a great deal of insight into how best to cope with and manage these inhibitory and executive problems. These are also set forth in this tidy little book in ways that are easily understood and implemented, especially now that one knows "why" they have to be done. Now we know why ADHD is the way it is and impairs people the way it does. And this is what makes this book on ADHD in adults so different from many others and so valuable to its reader. The most radical changes in our perspective often come from the most brief, simple, yet elegant explanations of things. Once we can grasp the logic of a theory or point of view, rivers of implications flow creating an ocean's worth of understanding from so humble an origin. Prepare for a paradigm shift; you will never see ADHD the same way again.

Russell A. Barkley, Ph.D.
Clinical Professor of Psychiatry
Medical University of South Carolina
Charleston, SC
And
Research Professor of Psychiatry
SUNY Upstate Medical University
Syracuse, NY

# Acknowledgments

My interest in the area of ADHD has developed over the last 18 years, beginning when I started to follow the work of Dr. Russell A. Barkley. Since then, Dr. Barkley has been acting as a colleague, a mentor, and a friend. Dr. Barkley's theory of self-control (1997) inspired me to write a text so that adults ADHD would understand the core of their impairments in their daily lives. Thus, without Dr. Barkley's research and theory, this book would not have been created.

The dream to write a book for adults with ADHD originated from my private practice in Florida, where I work with children, adolescents, and adults with ADHD. A great source of inspiration, information, and stimulation to write this book came from presentations and exchanges that I had with the North Broward Chapter of CHADD (Children and Adults with Attention Deficit Hyperactivity Disorder), a local support group for adults with ADHD in Coral Springs, Florida. I would like to thank the group coordinator, Annette Tabor, and the people who shared their experiences with me.

Lorie M. Wolf, Stephen Sherman, Juliana Lipinski and Vivian Tempel were instrumental in supporting me and in believing in my project as it was created. I also appreciate the support of Dr. Harvey Parker whose experience in the field and guidance have helped me approach this job with determination, yet with a realistic approach.

I would like to thank Monica, my younger daughter, for co-writing, reviewing, and editing this book using her wonderful writing abilities, humor and creativity.

The great impact of the contribution of Margaret Scott to this book cannot be measured. Margaret's work, art, empathy, and understanding were what permitted this book to become more attractive and interesting for the reader. I thank Margaret for being patient with me, and for believing in our project.

Finally, I would like to thank my whole family in Brazil, and my two essential mentors and support system during most of my personal as well as professional life: Dr. Sandy Nett, and Dr. Robert Woody.

# Adults with ADHD

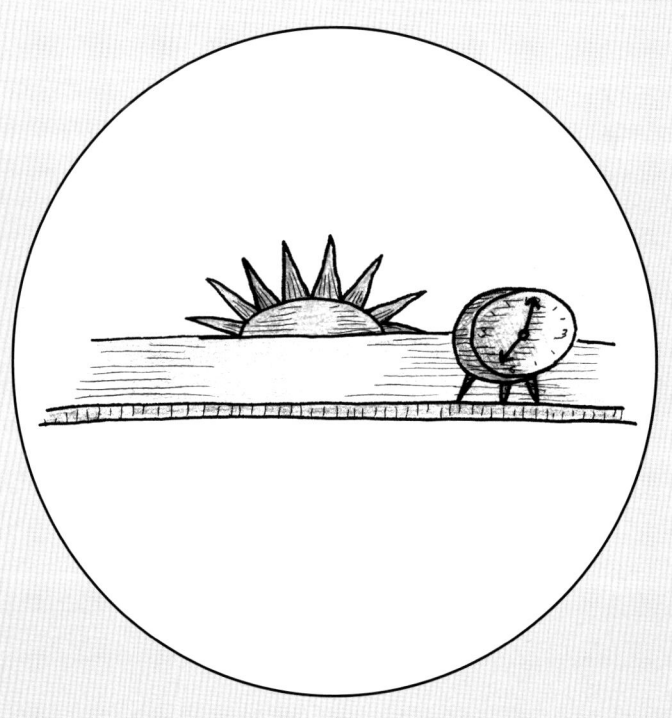

# A Day In The Life of An Adult With ADHD

## 1.The Purpose of This Book:

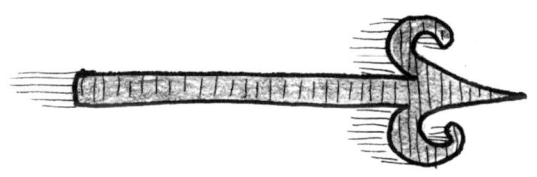

This book was developed as a tool for adults who have been diagnosed with ADHD. The intention of this book is to help adults like you develop strategies to deal with the difficulties associated with the recent diagnosis. These difficulties are not new to you. You have been living with them, and recognize the impediments in perspective of your disorder. The purpose of this book is to allow you to better understand and utilize the coping tools offered.

# 2. ADHD Across Life Span

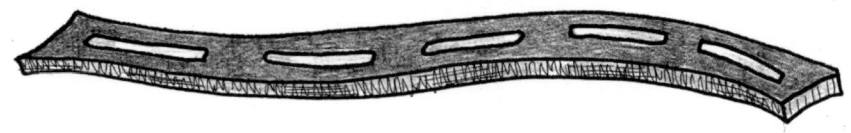

Attention Deficit/Hyperactivity Disorder, ADHD, is the most studied neurodevelopmental disorder (Wilens et al., 2002). Both health and scientific fields have recently recognized ADHD as a disorder that is chronic and persists in adulthood (Barkley, 2006).

According to recent research on the course and life of ADHD it appears that, as children develop into adolescence and adulthood, there are some changes in the way that the symptoms of ADHD are expressed. Symptoms of hyperactivity diminish and there is some decrease in impulsivity, but impairments in the areas of attention persist over time (Biederman, Mick, Faraone, 2000).

It is common for clinicians who work with children with ADHD to realize that there is also one parent who has ADHD, as ADHD is genetic at the rate of 80% (Barkley, 2006). When this happens, it is important to diagnose and treat the parent as part of the whole process of intervention with the child. This helps parents (adults) follow up with treatment recommendations for their children, such as giving medication, and learning and applying behavior management techniques in their daily family life. The rationale behind treating adults first (or at the same time as the children) can be explained by recalling what everyone hears when getting ready to take off on an airplane: "If you have an infant, please, be prepared to put on your Oxygen mask before putting on your child's."

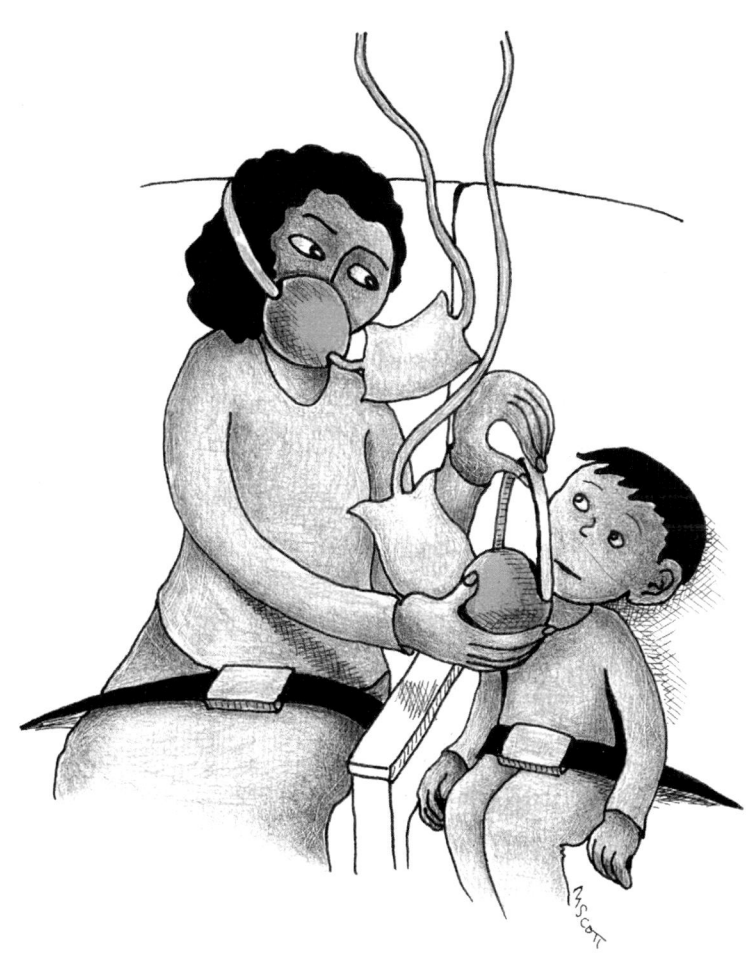

Parents who have ADHD find it difficult to adhere consistently to a treatment plan, may be inattentive during a parenting training program, and may forget to give their children medication as indicated (Barkley, 1997, Chronis et al., 2005). Therefore, helping the parent is vital not only for the benefit of the parent, but also as a step in the treatment of the child.

# 3. ADHD In Adults:

At this point, there is no one specific test to diagnose an adult with ADHD (Barkley, 2006). Conscientious clinicians should use a multi-method, multi-informant/setting battery of instruments. A basic assessment battery would include the following:

a. Interviewing the adult with the diagnosis of ADHD;
b. Obtaining developmental history, history of the impairment, and report cards from school, if possible;
c. Obtaining information from a collateral source, such as spouse, significant other, or parents;
d. Asking the patient (and the collateral source) to answer a few questionnaires (Barkley & Murphy, 2006) such as ADHD Self-Report Scales (Adler, Kessler, & Spencer, 2003), the Brown ADD scales (Brown, 1996) as well as others that have been developed more recently;
e. If necessary, giving some tests that measure "executive functions", such as "working memory", "reaction time", and "processing speed".

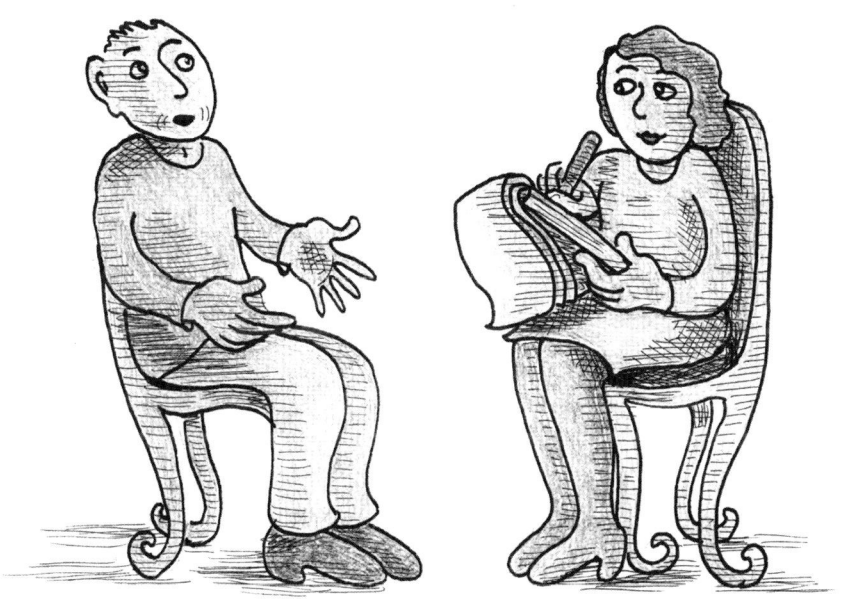

It is very important to use the services of a clinician who is trained in all areas of psychopathology and in ADHD because quite often ADHD in adults is accompanied by many other conditions (called co morbidity), such as Depression, Bipolar Disorder, Anxiety disorders, Drug Abuse and Addiction, and Antisocial Disorders.

This book is limited to explaining the difficulties that adults with ADHD encounter based on the impairments originated by this disorder only. Coping mechanisms to address other specific symptoms such as depression, anxiety, and obsessive-compulsive symptoms can be read in alternative sources, and these coping mechanisms can be worked on with a therapist.

# 4. How Does ADHD Iinterfere In An Adult's Life On An Every Day Basis?

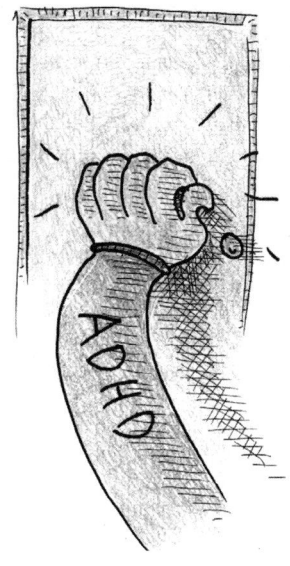

Adults with ADHD experience chronic difficulties during their entire day and night, with impairments in many environments, impacting their emotional, social, occupational, and physical well being.

What are the impairments that adults with ADHD have in all those environments, and with all the people involved in their lives? How are they expressed?

As children with ADHD grow older, the course of their symptoms changes. They usually become less hyperactive and at times less impulsive, but inattention persists. Here are some examples of how those difficulties are expressed:

1. Adults have what we call "cognitive" difficulties: For instance, they are inattentive (have a hard time sustaining attention in meeting, reading, and doing paper work), and may be easily

distracted or bored. Because of this, they tend to shift activities quite often, are less efficient due to poor time management, and may often lose things as a result of disorganization.

2.  Adults with ADHD may also have some hyperactivity. They may fidget, be overly talkative, and have sleep problems. For instance, it may be hard for an adult with ADHD to attend a classical concert or to sit through a movie or a long meeting at work without fidgeting.

3.  Adults with ADHD are often impulsive. Adults who are impulsive often display low frustration tolerance, temper outbursts, and impatience or irritability. Impulsivity may result in such outcomes as a person quitting (or losing) jobs or ending relationships quickly. There is also evidence of these impulsive adults having a more addictive personality.

According to Dr. Barkley's theory of self-control, ADHD is, above all else, a deficit of behavior inhibition. People who have ADHD have difficulty developing strategies to inhibit behaviors.

The term "behavioral inhibition" can have three meanings (Barkley, 1997):

(a) The ability to withhold a response, to not react impulsively, to delay responding: For instance, the ability to speak in public only at the right time; being careful to wait for the traffic light to turn green before you cross an intersection.

(b). The ability to stop an ongoing response (perseveration): To stop looking at the internet when you have to get ready for work, to stop working on a puzzle when a spouse calls you to have dinner.

(c) To resist distraction or disruption of performance of compet ing events: To not stop working when you hear your co-workers talking in the corridor of your office; to not stop researching online when a pop-up ad tries to claim your attention.

SELF CONTROL

Having the ability to inhibit behaviors is what helps us do all the tasks mentioned above, and this is an ability that develops from childhood. Children with ADHD have impairment in inhibiting behaviors, and as a consequence have impairments in certain brain functions that people use in their everyday life. Those functions, executive functions, are the skills used to help regulate and control behaviors.

Imagine a very busy, important CEO. We'll call her Ms. Worksalot. She has an executive secretary to take care of her schedule and to organize her work, appointments, meetings, trips, and vacations. Ms. Worksalot's secretary helps her with time management and scheduling, completing and filing important paperwork, making appointments, preparing for meetings, and paying bills. Her secretary also calls her to wake her up in the morning, even telling her which clothes to wear and which shoes match. The secretary calls the CEO to ask if she is running on time in and out of the shower and in eating breakfast, and tells her about her first appointment. The secretary calls her every hour of every day, and also schedules long-term events, such as annual doctor and dentist's appointments.

All people have to use their organizational skills, thinking as if they were their own executive secretaries. When we use these executive functions, we are able to internalize behaviors. Thus, we learn from experience, and we are able to anticipate what happens when our environment changes.

From the minute we are born, we are always learning from our environment. By using behavioral inhibition, self-control, and executive functions, we are able to deal with changes that happen in our environment. In which situations is it important for us to use executive functions?

1. When we have to do something with the expectation of out comes (rewards) in the future;
2. When we have to focus on some kind of work, and keep our selves from paying attention to more interesting, exciting things;
3. When we need to use a whole sequence of behaviors and actions in order to reach our goal.

All the above situations require us to inhibit other behaviors, to stay focused on a task, and to delay gratification until a later time All people with ADHD (children and adults) have a difficult time developing these skills.

There are many areas of executive functions that are impaired in children and adults with ADHD. Understanding these impairments is vital to coping with ADHD. In this book, we will briefly review these areas of difficulty.

1. **Working memory**: the ability to hold events in mind, and to act upon the events. (For example: to control a motor response.)

For instance, what is your routine in the morning? If you have a set routine, you have developed a sequence of behaviors, and knowing how long each of them takes allows you to be on time for work.

Adults with ADHD may have difficulty in learning sequences of behaviors and gauging how long they take to be completed. As a consequence, they often do not learn from experience. Thinking, "I can squeeze in another stop to pick up the clothes at the cleaners before my appointment, and I will make it on time", (when actually they are already late for that appointment) is something quite common for adults with ADHD.

Not having a sense of time, or what Dr. Barkley calls "myopia of time" (1997) creates many challenges in the life of adults with ADHD. In addition to often being late, adults with ADHD also have a difficult time waiting, whether for movie tickets, a table in a restaurant, or the subway. For an adult with ADHD, 10 minutes is a long time. Why? Because adults with ADHD perform better if they receive rewards for their behavior immediately, thus waiting is difficult because they don't have a sense of time, a sense of "window of time" (Barkley, 1997).

When someone does not have a sense of time, and cannot hold sequences of behaviors in working memory, it is very difficult to develop a repertoire of behaviors, and to learn from this. Thus, an adult with ADHD may not learn from experience that the extra cup of coffee before going to work did make him late the past 5 days. He continues getting to work late. This adult has trouble seeing that his late arrival for work is a consequence of his stop for coffee. The inability to connect experiences is a prime example of myopia of time, and of working memory problems.

Also, it is difficult to make plans for the future if someone does not learn from past experiences! How can you know what steps to take to reach a final goal, which behaviors to display, and how long it will take, if you do not remember your experiences the previous trials?

One experience with the above situations can be illustrated with the story of a young adult, "Outofsightandmind", who has been aware of having ADHD since a very young age. When he was asked about previous trips and vacations, he said that he did not remember them. Of course, "Outofsightandmind" never carried a camera in his pocket. He also did not recall how he celebrated his first 25 birthdays… Merely recommending that he use a camera to mark important memories gave him a chance to feel the impact of keeping memories. We offered an EXTERNAL TOOL to help him develop memory for the successful and important events in his life, and to stress the development of ways to internalize such experiences.

2. **Internalization of Speech**: The idea of working memory also has some implications for the development of language. Adults with ADHD often talk to themselves and have a difficult time solving a problem without speaking it aloud. Adults with ADHD have less developed "self-speech." Environmental factors and immediate rewards compete with internal language and morals in controlling their behavior.

This conflict may lead adults with ADHD to make decisions impulsively, even though they have experienced negative consequences for such decisions in the past.

3. **Self-regulation of affect**: Children and adults with ADHD also have difficulty regulating and controlling their emotions. In general, people are internally motivated to do most things. However, people with ADHD are dependent on the environment to be motivated to complete tasks, especially if those activities are repetitive, boring, or present long-term rewards.

Without self-regulation of affect, people may react to events in an inappropriate manner or at an inopportune time, such as exploding to bad news in the middle of a business meeting. This also applies to positive emotions. For instance, when you receive a bonus at work and are very happy, you may want to brag and let the whole world know, but you may not do it when you think about the appropriateness of that behavior, that it may make other employees jealous or uncomfortable. People with ADHD have more difficulty repressing both unhappy and ecstatic outbursts.

4. **Reconstitution**: All the above skills allow people to analyze and learn about behaviors and the implication and consequences of these behaviors. This involves analyzing and synthesizing behavior, or taking the behaviors apart, and putting them together in an organized way. As Dr. Barkley puts it, "reconstitution is the ability to take apart and rapidly recom-

bine information (images, words, behavior) into new arrangements in order to discover new strategies and solve problems as you go through life" (2004, personal communication). This dissection of behavior also allows people to develop morals, principles for their behavior, and to learn general rules.

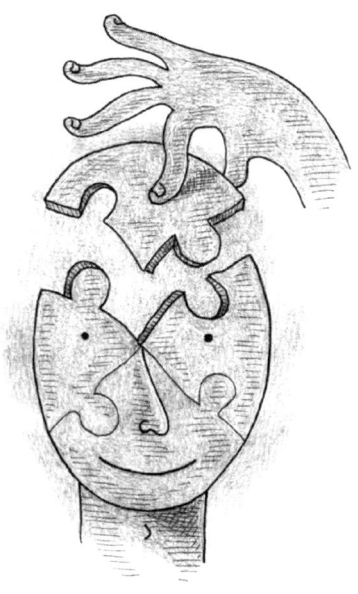

How easily and smoothly you can do all of the skills above is what Dr. Barkley calls fluency of behavior (1997). This important skill entails adjusting the content of one's speech and behavior to each situation, recognizing the need to adapt, and ably doing so. For instance, the ability to be able to speak in front of a group of professionals about your field of work, and then to explain the same information to a group of children who are interested in your profession requires you to put the information together in a different way.

All the above skills allow people to live in an environment where they use their repertoire of behaviors, their memories, and the control of their emotions to relate to their world, and the people in it, in a healthy, constructive, and positive way.

29

At this point you have achieved the important first step of awareness and understanding of the impairment of adults with ADHD. Knowing "what" is a huge part, but nothing changes unless you then know how to harness your new knowledge and improve your life. Knowing that you may mess up your desk and then, distracted, leave it that way is not much help, is it? In this book we will attempt to provide you with coping strategies and specific suggestions which you can personalize and apply to your lifestyle needs in order to develop routines and tools that will alter the impact of impairment in your life.

Though medication is often prescribed for ADHD and is the number one treatment tool for this condition, it is just one part of a multi-faceted approach to progress in the right direction. Developing a support system of loved ones who understand your disorder and who can help you apply the suggestions made within this book may enable you to bring your life closer to the life you imagine for yourself in a disorder-free world.

In the next chapter, we will make some suggestions of coping mechanisms that adults with ADHD may use to deal with their daily difficulties. These suggestions are based on two major principles, which we will summarize below.

There are two main elements on which to focus when developing strategies for adults with ADHD:

1. As we mentioned above, adults with ADHD know WHAT they need to do, but the challenge comes with regards to when they do it, and how they go about doing the "boring, repetitive tasks." Thus, one needs to focus on the following:

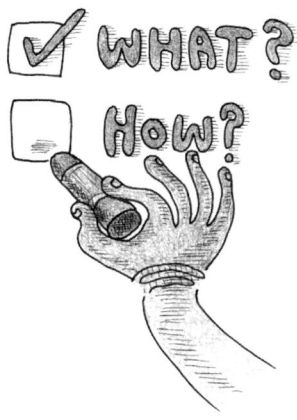

**WHEN AND HOW** to persist on doing what needs to be done.

2. A second basic principle that guides behaviors of people with ADHD is that they are more likely to behave in a way that will lead to immediate rewards rather than long term ones. Additionally, an external reward is much more powerful than internal motivation.

Thus, taking the two above principles into consideration, the ideal strategy to develop to help adults with ADHD complete daily tasks needs to focus not only on immediate consequences for behaviors, but also on employing external rewards. Therefore, we will make suggestions on how to develop immediate consequences and reminders for series of behaviors that are boring, repetitive, and nonrewarding by themselves, and how to impose external rewards contingent upon the behaviors' completion. Introducing external reminders and external rewards can help you complete the boring, repetitive, uninteresting tasks such as paying bills, completing paper work, and remembering to call customers as a follow-up for business.

In order to be more aware of time, have frequent reminders of sequences of behaviors that you must complete. Bear this in mind as we now use our newly gained tools and examine how to improve the typical day of an adult with ADHD.

Taking into account the key concepts noted above, in the next chapter we will make some suggestions on how to develop external and immediate rewards in situations in your daily life that are boring, repetitive, and not immediately gratifying to you.

# A Day in the Life...

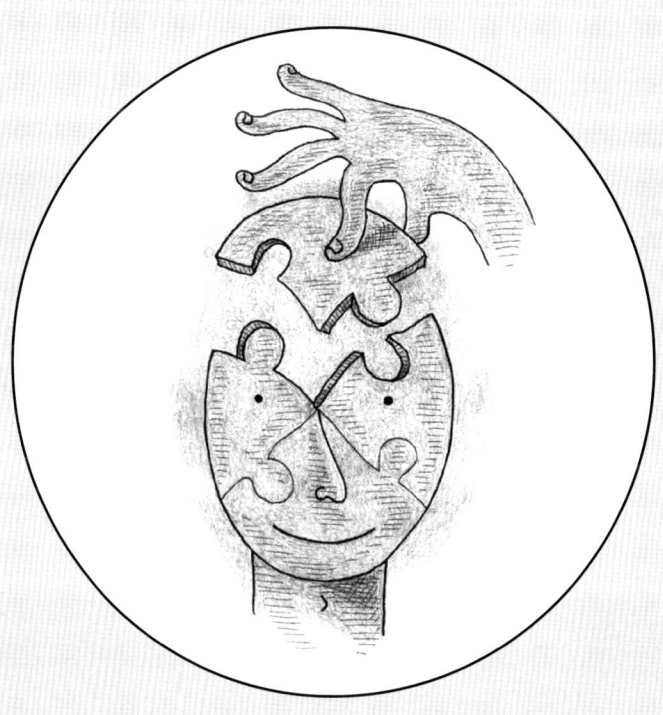

This chapter will present challenges you may encounter during the events of a typical day, and introduce what we have found to be useful tools in addressing the obstacles you as an adult with ADHD may face.

## 1. Wake Up

How often do you think that your alarm clock did not work, then realize that you pressed snooze on the alarm clock and don't remember? This is a frequent occurrence, and our experience has taught us that one way to solve this problem is to buy cheap, noisy alarm clocks, and to put two or three of them in various areas of your bedroom and even bathroom and kitchen, not only by your bed. If one fails, you still have the others. And, more importantly, the alarm clocks force immediate compliance, as you have to get out of bed immediately to turn them off.

## 2. Morning Shower

People with ADHD have difficulty with management of time, and often forget about life obligations while they take a shower. Most people, even those who don't belt ballads into their shampoo bottles, get distracted by this potentially relaxing time. So, having an alarm clock or a kitchen timer in the bathroom to help you time your shower has been an idea welcomed by adults with ADHD.

Continuing the use of the timer while you get dressed, have breakfast, and read the paper in the morning before going to work may help you in imposing an external modulator and reminder of time. With practice, you may get used to a routine that will help you internalize the management of time for this important beginning of your day.

## 3. Getting Ready To Leave The House

Prepare as much as possible the day before. It is helpful to get your clothes ready the previous night. Also, make your lunch (and the children's snacks and lunches) the night before. Why? Doing so will diminish your sequence of morning behaviors, and you will find fewer distracters from your necessary routine. This also allows you flexibility for these behaviors, letting you spend more time selecting your shoes before an important day or cutting the crust off your daughter's sandwich, without feeling as much stress for time as you might have in the morning.

## 4. Driving To Work

Make sure that you also have a set routine and route going from home to work, or home to school to drop off children, and then to work. It is best not to include any "novelty" in that routine. Any new element in that routine may only include more challenges in many areas, such as distractions, time management problems, and more demands on your organizational skills. If you must add variety, allow yourself two or three routes, but assign each route specifically to the same day each week, thus making it a permanent part of each day's routine, and also reminding you each morning which specific day of the week it is.

For the potential problems a deviation from routine can cause, let us look at Dani, a fictional character.

Dani takes his children to school every day before going to work at the Law Office. Dani has clients every day at 9 o'clock. With the help of his therapist, wife, and coach, Dani finally got used to his routine in the morning, and was able to make it to the office at about 8:50 a.m. every day, allowing him to be on time for work.

On Dani's daughter's 5th birthday, the family had planned to celebrate her birthday after school and work by going for pizza in the evening with the grandparents. However, when Dani's daughter got in the car that morning, she asked her father if he would stop and get some donuts since it was her birthday. Dani looked at his watch, and said: "O.K., today we can do that, since it's your birthday, and we will celebrate the whole day!"

Dani, the birthday girl, and her brother stopped for donuts. There were about 20 types of donuts, and various drink choices. Dani read all the choices for the kids, enjoying the variety of colors and shapes and flavors of donuts offered. Time went by. The kids did not want to eat in the car, so the three of them had their donuts in the shop. When Dani looked at his watch, it was already 8:50! The kids got to school late, and Dani was half an hour late for his new client.

As you see, once we forget about time, it is hard to go back to keeping track of it.

We don't mean to suggest that you, as an adult with ADHD, need to be so rigid about your time and your life, or that you are not allowed variety or enjoyment. However, since time presents one of the major impairments, you need to be constantly checking to make sure that you don't lose track of it, and to discover your own best methods of regulation and reminders.

## 5. Work Performance, and Peer Relationships

Keep track of your organizational skills and how you maintain your work area. Of course you know that you need to keep your desk in order, and that you need to keep your appointments in order, and to be on time for them, but how can you go about doing all of these things?

Some suggestions may be to find creative ways to impose external reminders in a way that ensures that you will complete those very boring, repetitious, and tedious tasks immediately.

For instance, having a peer remind you, or help you with some of the organizational skills may be helpful. One good example happened when two people from a CHADD (Children and Adults with Attention Deficit/Hyperactivity Disorder) Adult Support group decided to help each other in organizing their desks. They would meet once a month and the two of them would go to each other's office and clean up their desks. To reward themselves, they would go out for coffee afterwards. This, for them was a creative solution which allowed for socializing and enjoyment even as it imposed an external routine to help organization.

This example shows a real life application of the principles discussed in this book:
- (a) Impose external reminders (have a set date and the presence of another adult to help persist on a task);
- (b) Do it at a specific time (once a month, remind each other of the time),
- (c) And reward yourself for the completion of the behavior afterwards (immediate reward of behavior with a cup of coffee)

By following these principles, adults with ADHD can start to better organize their lives.

Let's look at the story of our fictional character, Stuart:

Stuart is an adult with ADHD. He did well in school up until high school. However, his "citizenship" notes on his report card in elementary school were not as good as his grades. Stuart had a difficult time sitting still, interrupted other children, did not finish his work, and was often called out by the teacher to pay more attention to the lessons. Stuart went through high school with C's, although all his teachers thought he had greater potential.

After graduating from a state college with degrees in business and mathematics, Stuart started working in the area of sales. He loved making contact with new customers, engaging them in learning about his product, and selling his product to them. Stuart became very well known by his customers, but when he had to follow-up his sales activities with paper work, and with phone calls (to ensure that the customers liked the products, and that they were working well), Stuart did not do so well. Slowly, he started getting negative feedback from his manager, and he lost significant contracts with buyers due to the lack of follow-up phone calls.

The above situation is very common with adults with ADHD.

Stuart has a gift in contacting and engaging customers to buy his product. However, when he has to complete more boring, repetitive, and nonstimulating tasks, Stuart does not perform well, postpones those activities, or even forgets about them.

What are some of the suggestions that one may have to help Stuart with his difficulties associated with symptoms of ADHD?

Stuart may want to use all kinds of reminders to externally remind him of his obligations, such as calling customers every week. He may allocate a specific time of the day to do those tedious tasks, such as right before lunch. By doing this, Stuart can use lunch as a reward for the completion of such tasks.

No matter what the details of one's work, the principle is the same. Allocating a specific time to complete the tedious work is a way to help remind oneself of completing a task. Also, having an alarm or noise from a computer, palm pilot, or other device is helpful, but only if you complete the task right after the alarm goes off, and you manage to find a way to amiably apologize to your coworkers for the noise pollution.

The alarm or visual reminder will help you go about doing the task, but the fact remains that you have to do the task yourself. Developing lists to remind yourself of your obligations and tasks for the day are helpful only if you complete them the instant you look at the reminder or hear the alarm.

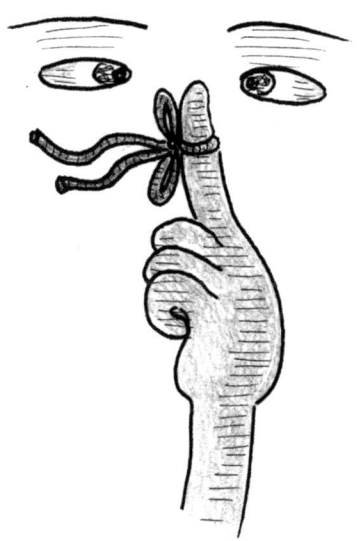

Let us talk about another example of Ms. OpenArt, an experienced art teacher at a small school. She is very creative, well liked by her students, and the content and format of her classes are very rich and innovative. However, Ms. OpenArt is on probation with the principal due to her lack of organization in her messy classroom and her delay in turning in grades and evaluations of students. She was also asked to create an art club, into which she put a lot of work. However, Ms. OpenArt did not accomplish the goal of developing a program to visit various museums and art galleries in the area. Although this teacher really wanted to do all of the above, she did not find time, and was always planning the visits in her mind, yet never put the proposal on paper to be approved by the committee at school.

Further, the administration was also aware that Ms. OpenArt was very verbal in the teacher's lounge. She often shared her personal life with teachers and other staff members of the school to the point that she would not stop talking with faculty members of the staff about details of her dating life. Some of the teachers were starting to feel uncomfortable with the situation, thinking that Ms OpenArt had difficulty with boundaries in the workplace. In addition, Ms. OpenArt would start talking with a peer in the teacher's lounge, forget about time, and arrive late for her classes.

How could Ms. OpenArt use the principles and strategies we discussed to solve her difficulties?

Ms OpenArt could ask one of her colleagues to help her organize her. She could ask Mr. MathPerfect, the "neat freak" Geometry teacher, to help her clean her room once a month. In return, she could promise to cook a gourmet meal for him or draw him a painting to hang in his classroom, for example.

Other strategies for Ms. OpenArt would be to have a calendar, which she could create with her artistic background, with reminders to plan for events by specific dates. She would allocate time to write and plan such events on the same days of the week. For instance, when Ms. OpenArt had a break in between two classes, she could dedicate that time to tedious paperwork. Also, she could plan her grading system quite in advance so that she would not be so late turning in the grades.

Once Ms OpenArt realized how her openness with staff members was negatively impacting her relationship with her peers, she chose to talk about her personal life only with the people who were closer to her, and not during work, instead meeting her best friend for coffee once a week. Ms. OpenArt also had a conversation with the administrator in which they addressed her difficulties and both agreed to be more constructive and open in order to prevent problems from escalating.

The two examples above represent just a slice of the challenges that the demands of work present to an adult with ADHD. It is important to look at the characteristics of your job, your routine, your daily life, and the particular demands placed on your executive functions specifically. For instance, for an adult who still has significant impulsivity and hyperactivity (there are some), a "desk job" is not ideal. In addition, some people do not work well in cubicles due to the high level of noise and distractions. Recognizing that environmental noises may distract you at work may help you develop a more suitable environment for your work to be more productive.

Many adults with ADHD like to work in jobs that are less attached to a schedule. For instance, they may want to work in writing late at night or in sales over the computer (around the clock), and not have to be tied to a schedule or physical location.

It would be ideal to be able to choose the perfect job for each individual in the world of work. However, all types of jobs still have boundaries, such as productivity, time management, and demands for demonstration of work and efficiency. All those measures of work and success depend on one's use of executive functions.

## 6. After Work

It would be helpful to end your day of work celebrating what you have accomplished. Also, look at your calendar- check the tasks that you completed, and write down the ones you did not in order to make sure that you complete them the next day (if this is the case).

Reexamining your progress is a necessary step to take frequently during the day and at night. This will help you start the next day with a plan.

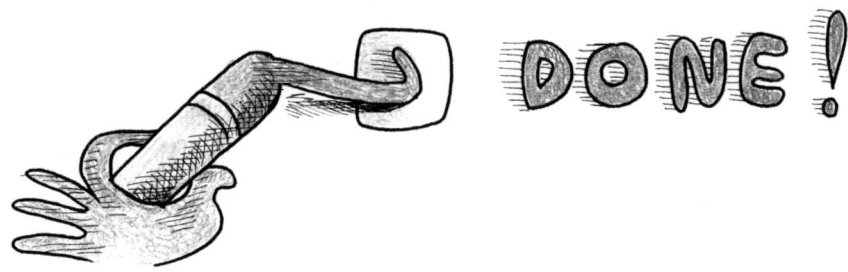

Leave yourself a few minutes to clean your work area. This can give you a sense of completion and the feeling that tomorrow you will start fresh, and can be a very important boost. No matter what type of work you do, this is a therapeutic and practical action that you may want to include in your schedule.

## 7. The Commute Home

Perhaps now is the time during which you can allow yourself variety, stress release, or relaxation. Maybe one day you can afford to be more flexible with your time, and stop somewhere in between work and home (or your next stop). For instance, you may want to ask your spouse to pick up the children at school so that you can just relax or exercise before going home a couple of days a week. Of course, only you know your schedule, and you have to be realistic and adjust the recommendations to your daily life. If you have time deadlines after work as well, continue your practices of keeping an eye on your watch or alarm clock even when you take a short post-work relaxation break. Do not get so carried away at the sauna at the gym that you forget your nightly family meeting, your daughter's ballet rehearsal, or to be on time to pick up your wife at the airport.

No matter what your weekly schedule is, it is important to be aware of time management. In order to achieve all the goals during the week, keep reminders of your time, and try to not distract your-self from your step-by-step routine.

## 8. At Home and With Family

It is vital to schedule a specific time to do chores like going to the bank, grocery shopping, and doing laundry. In doing that, you don't even have to think about it, it will be on your schedule, in your palm pilot, and on your calendar at home (of course, you need to write all of that down in the beginning so that you remember what days you have to do specific chores, especially the boring ones.)

Delegate chores and activities and ask others to help you and to remind you. If you live with your family, you may ask your significant other to be your "coach", and to remind you of your boring chores. By asking them to do that, you will not be offended if they actually remind you (to take out the garbage, walk the dog, etc). Also, you may want to delegate some activities to your spouse, or to the other significant people in your home and social life.

How about paying bills? This activity is something so common yet still creates tremendous stress and fights in families. For an adult with ADHD, paying bills is one of the most boring, tedious, non-rewarding tasks one could ever do. There is no immediate reward in paying bills; actually, there is a long-term punishment if one does not pay bills (fines, disconnected services, low credit). As a matter of fact, there are people who still do not organize paying their bills even after their electricity and telephone services are disconnected.

By using the principles of immediacy, external reminder, delegating, and external imposition of time management and organization, you can develop strategies to use your executive functions.

Let us use the example of fictional ADHD adult Mr. Doitlater. Due to a recent change in his job, Mr. Doitlater arrives at home before his wife every day. Because of this, Mr. "Doitlater" now collects the mail everyday. He would take the mail from the mailbox, put it on the dinner table, (or wherever else he stopped) and leaf half heartedly through the envelopes. Usually, Mr. Doitlater would open only the envelope that he did not recognize (novelty is more exciting, and catches one's attention more quickly).

Mr. Doitlater forgot where he put the mail one day, but continued to think that he put all of it on the dinner table. After a couple of weeks, his wife asked him whether he had paid the electricity bill. Mr. Doitlater looked at the many piles on the dinner table, but only found old newspapers.

Their family went through tremendous stress trying to find and pay the bills. How can a family like that organize their mail and bills in order to pay them on time and keep a record of their payments?

Having a set place for the mail is important. Knowing where the mail always is and putting it in a chronological folder would help the couple sit down on a specific day once a week and pay all the bills that are due at once.

Always put mail in the same place, and impose an external management of time for paying the bills. Delegating or paying the bills together with a spouse or another responsible adult also helps as a way to remind oneself of what to do. If you live alone, ask a friend to remind you to sit down every week at the same time (or write yourself a note you know you will see). Other tasks for the house and family are similar to the one described above.

## 9. Social Life, Rituals, Holidays:

Mr. Allover asked Ms. Attentive on a date. They had met a couple of times before with other friends, and he wanted to take her out for dinner to get to know her better, because he had a feeling he really liked her.

Mr. Allover picked Ms. Attentive up at her door, but he was 45 minutes late to meet her because he stopped to get her some flowers, and he took a long time to pick the perfect bouquet for her. Knowing how late he was, Mr. Allover drove a little too fast on the way to Ms. Attentive's house, and he got a ticket for speeding. Poor Mr. Allover! Once he picked up his date, they drove to a restaurant. Mr. Allover chose a nice, casual sports bar to help them be more comfortable on their first date. The couple found a table and ordered. Mr. Allover started talking about his week, his job, and the drama of the ticket he had just gotten, and Ms. Attentive listened attentively. He also apologized for being so late to pick her up. When she began to tell him that it was understandable, Mr. Allover realized that he was having some difficulty paying attention to Ms. Attentive. He had three television sets surrounding him, and they were showing his favorite basketball team playing on TV! He could not control himself. He kept looking up to find out the score of the game. The date ended up being a disaster. Mr. Allover felt very bad about his behavior and was so embarrassed that he never asked Ms. Attentive on a date again.

53

If you are planning to go out to eat with a date, your spouse, a child, or anyone just to talk, make sure the environment is not distracting for you. Sports bars, very busy restaurants, even window seats may not be the most ideal locations.

Paying attention to your social skills is also very important, such as how loud you are, how impulsive you are, whether you are able to actually listen to someone speak and then respond to their statements, or whether you are already thinking of what you are going to say next.

Asking your close friends to give you feedback on your social behaviors may help you tremendously in your encounters with people. Also, making sure that you arrive at places on time for your social endeavors is important, and the strategies used are the same as we described above for your work schedule.

While on the topic of maintaining social relationships and stability in relationship life, another useful strategy is to keep notes (even short ones) for events that repeat themselves every year. For instance, if a person keeps track of when he started getting presents for the holiday, how long it took, and how much money he spends during the months of November and December, he will be able to look at those notes next year, at the same time. By doing this, one is externalizing his/her experience, and can learn from that experience. Another example is a person who keeps track of the shopping list, expenses, time to organize a house, the table, and the cooking for a very sophisticated dinner, such as Thanksgiving, Christmas, or Passover. A final example is keeping a permanent wall calendar with everyone's birthdays that you make sure to check daily. Checking every morning can become a mindless ritual, but will ensure that you do not forget anyone's birthday. You can even make it a habit to buy presents exactly a weekend ahead of time so that you are always prepared, and are comfortable with your routine.

## 9. Education

Important people in your life may know that you have ADHD, and that it is a disability. In addition to this knowledge, it is vital that you and your significant other and family members make the effort to learn and educate yourselves about ADHD, ADHD in adults, and how it affects your life and the lives of everyone around you.

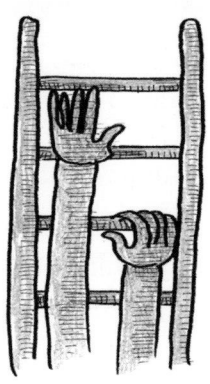

Reading books and having a support team of professionals working with you, such as your physician (who may prescribe medication for your symptoms), your therapist (if you need one), coach, and your family are crucial. Also, attending meetings, workshops, and support groups can be very helpful.

Two nonprofit organizations, the Children and Adults with Attention Deficit Disorder (CHADD), and the Attention Disorder Association (ADDA) are good examples of the value of support groups for adults and children. Groups can develop a solid interaction about their success stories and the coping mechanisms they used in situations of stress at work, at home, and in their personal lives. For instance, in a local chapter, one adult used the help of another to clean her house, and in return invited that person to a holiday meal. The group also developed a list of coping skills and success stories that they shared at a National Meeting of the CHADD organization. Spouses of the adults with ADHD also went to the meetings, and became involved with the organization.

The support groups are even more critical for single mothers and single people who do not have family close by to support them. The sense of solidarity and hearing stories and coping tools from others can be a great help to all those with the disorder.

## 10. Health

Last but not least, health is a very important aspect of the life of an adult with ADHD. All people need to make sure that they are leading a healthy life, but the adult with ADHD often forgets to make appointments with doctors and dentists for checkups, semi-annual visits, mammography, and other necessary exams.

Weekly and daily health related habits are also part of the recommendations in this book. For instance, having an external reminder to exercise (like a peer to go to the gym with you after work), preparing healthy lunches for the next day (so that one does not have to rush through a drive through window at a fast food restaurant), and attempting a balanced life can be ways to avoid less beneficial results of impulsive decisions.

Since adults with ADHD may have more difficulty falling asleep, it is also important to avoid drinking large amounts of caffeine on a typical night. Moreover, taking care of other health related conditions associated with the ADHD, such as depression, anxiety, mood conditions, or any other aspects of your health and mind, is an integral step in ensuring a happier lifestyle.

Finally, more recent studies show that adults with ADHD who do not treat the disorder appropriately are more likely to get into situations that are of great risk for their lives. These may include using and abusing drugs and alcohol more often, getting into car accidents (Cox et al., 2004) that are also more serious (Barkley, 2005), or receiving speeding tickets. In addition, there is higher incidence of educational drop outs and poorer occupational and social adjustment within the ADHD population (Fischer et al., 2005). Moreover, there are more cases of unplanned pregnancy, sexual promiscuity, and higher incidence of venereal diseases in this population as well (Fischer et. al., 2005). Untreated adults with ADHD are also more likely to display depression, and have lower ability to function as a parent (Chronis et al., 2005, Chronis et al., in press, Jensen, 2004).

The above results found in recent research simply accentuate the need to diagnose and treat ADHD in adults. It also underscores the need to develop a support system that will help the adult stay healthy in all areas of physical, emotional, and social well being, as well as remaining educationally aware and financially stable.

## 11. CONCLUSION

We hope that in the last two chapters you were able to become familiar with the sources of difficulties that adults with ADHD may encounter in their daily lives, though in all likelihood, you do not need to be told about any of the troubles you live through on a daily basis. More importantly, we hope that you have learned the basic elements necessary to develop strategies to deal with the everyday struggles that one finds in dealing with chores, activities, work, family, and social as well as emotional life.

Provided is a form for you to complete to help you start developing strategies for your own life. Remember, it is important to develop ways to turn difficult, boring, and tedious situations into more immediate tasks with immediate rewards (or consequences).Use external reminders and rewards to help you actually perform the task as soon as you think of it so that you do not forget, or press your mental "snooze" button.

Form:

Date:

Time:

Where:

I have to do the following:

_____

_____

How can I use external reminders to help me remember, and to sustain doing the task?

_____

_____

Can I use any externally driven reward to complete my task thinking of a good consequence later?_____

_____

_____

Can I delegate my task, or part of it to someone in my environment? Or can I ask someone to be "with me", or "check on me" often to help me start the task, stay on task, and finish it?

_____
_____
_____
_____


Can I change the task? Or change the environment to make it more attractive and less distracting to me?_____
_____

Learning about the impairments of ADHD and using the tools described in this chapter are just a couple of necessary elements in dealing with ADHD. As previously mentioned, medical treatment is a vital tool in treating ADHD, as is behavior therapy. The next chapter will be dedicated to discussing treatments of ADHD, the logical and necessary step which follows recognizing the symptoms and learning coping mechanisms.

# How To Treat ADHD in Adults

In the previous chapters, we reviewed the fact that ADHD is a real condition in adults, and that it can have a significant negative impact on all areas of people's life: emotional, educational, social, professional, and health.

An adult with ADHD should treat this disorder the same way he would approach any medical disorder (such as diabetes): with ongoing and well managed treatment. Once an accurate diagnosis is completed, it is clear that medication is the first treatment of choice (Biederman, 2002).

In addition to medication, treatment of ADHD in adults is also focused on behavior modification, cognitive-behavior therapy (to address other symptoms, such as depression and anxiety). It is also important to incorporate the family in treatment, and to help them learn about the condition.

Most adults with ADHD have comorbidities (i.e., other disorders that happen with ADHD). The decision about what symptoms to treat first with medication and in therapy will depend on which symptoms impair the adult the most. For instance, the adult with ADHD who has very high levels of anxiety, not even able to leave the house, will be better treated for anxiety and ADHD, addressing the anxiety symptoms first, since these are keeping the individual from leaving his home, a drastic and pressing problem.

The presence of drug abuse and addiction also plays a role in the decision of how to treat the symptoms of ADHD (Wilens, 2004). At the same time, there is evidence that an accurate treatment of ADHD may diminish the risk of drug abuse (Biederman et al., 1999).

## A. Medications for ADHD

It is not within the scope of this book to review all the available medications for the treatment of ADHD. However, some recommendations will be made regarding the process of looking for the best medical treatment and follow-up regarding medication. The reader should refer to specific sources for more detailed information about the available medications for ADHD (Adler, L., 2006; Barkley, R.A., 2006, and www.myadhd.com ). At the end of this book there is a list of sources for your review. Once you read articles and other sources that are based on scientific research (not on opinions), you should go to your doctor and discuss the various medications available for adults with ADHD.

In discussing medication with your doctor, remember what you read in this book. An adult with ADHD goes through challenges during the whole day - from the morning, when he wakes up, until the evening, when he has to organize his personal, social, and family life. Thus, it would be helpful to remind your doctor that medications that have a sustained effect for an extended period of time during the day may be the best indication for you. Be open with your doctor as well, and only you know your body and your schedule best. It would be helpful to inform your doctor about the most difficult times of day for you both with regards to scheduling as well as attention problems.

There are some advantages of taking medication that lasts long periods of time:

1. An adult with ADHD often forgets daily tasks, and taking the medication is one of them. If he has to take it only once a day, he is less likely to forget to take his pill. This person will thus be more compliant with treatment, and have better results.

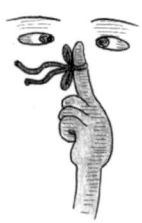

2.  Even if the adult remembers to take medication during the middle of the day, he may be at work, during a business lunch, talking on the telephone, or in the middle of completing a manual project. Taking medication at home in the morning keeps the adult's privacy, and it does not interfere with that person's relationship with peers and with work or itself become a distraction from other tasks.

3.  One dosage a day helps the person's activities during the whole day and into the evening.

4.  One dosage (or sometimes two, depending on the medication) may help the adult with driving in the evening going back home from work, when there may be a lot of traffic at that time of the day (in some cities). Note that, as previously mentioned, adults with ADHD are more likely to get traffic tickets, and to get into (more serious) accidents (Barkley et al., 2002). For some, the drive home may be a time which tries the patience, a dangerous time when even more attention and focus are mandatory.

5.  A young adult who is in college may benefit from long acting medication in order to help him with studying late at night, and also in making decisions about drinking, socializing, and other risky activities, such as abusing drugs and having unprotected sex.

It is crucial that you discuss with your doctor the benefits as well as the side effects of the medications of choice for ADHD. The physician will tell you that all medications may have potential side effects, but some of them are temporary, and there are ways to manage them.

## B. Medication management for ADHD

It is very important to know that all studies conducted in the area of ADHD in adults provided results for large groups of people. Each individual needs to consult with the doctor to decide whether it is important to have any exams completed before taking the medication under consideration. Although you are the "patient", you need to have an active role in helping the doctor decide on what medication you will take, as well as the dosage. These are some points to consider when you are starting to take medication:

a.  Once the doctor decides which medication to prescribe to you, he/she will explain the effects, the benefits, and possible side effects of the medication. He/she will explain the dosages, and whether you will have to increase the dosage with time, and when to do it.

b.  You need to be open with the doctor when it comes to having other symptoms, such as depression, bipolar disorder, drug and alcohol abuse and dependency, among other health issues.

c.  The doctor may take some time to decide the best dosage of the medication for you, and you need to be patient with the doctor, and give him/her feedback on every dosage-stage.

d.  Prepare a list of questions to ask your doctor on a frequent basis, and take that list to your appointment. Do not be shy to ask questions, because the more you know about the medication you are taking, the more you will be able to give relevant information to your doctor, and you will benefit more from treatment. Questions will provide you with necessary information, and may include the following as well as others:

- What are the side effects of this medication?
- How do I know that this is the best dosage for me?
- How do I know that this is the best medication for me?
- Can I take other medications?
- Can I drink any alcohol with this medication?
- What should I do if I miss a dose?
- Do I need to take this with food?

e. Finally, it would be good to keep track of the improvement of your symptoms with an objective scale for adults with ADHD.

## C. Psychotherapy

As mentioned before, it is common for an adult with ADHD who has never been treated appropriately (with medication) for ADHD to have other disorders also, such as anxiety, depression, low self-esteem, and drug abuse. Because of that, it is possible that your doctor may give you more than one medication to address all your symptoms. The doctor will treat what is impairing your life most, such as the emotional, social, and occupational areas in your life.

At the same time, there is research evidence that cognitive-behavioral therapy also helps the adult with ADHD. It would help to center therapy in the areas that we described in this book, such as organization, to develop a routine with external and immediate rewards as much as possible.

Therapy can also help you deal with the negative consequences of your impulsive behaviors, lack of motivation, low self-esteem, problems with relationships, with work, with health, and with the family. Also, involving the family in therapy, and teaching them about ADHD and the implications of this condition in your lives may help you develop a support system and also decrease conflict in your significant relationships, such as with couples and with other members of the family.

Finally, going to local C.H.A.D.D. and A.D.D.A. meetings may help you and your family learn more, share, and find support from organizations that educate and advocate for people with ADHD, as well as giving you a group of understanding peers to consult and with which you may feel comfortable.

## D. Epilogue

We hope that in this chapter we have provided you with information on treatment of ADHD. It is important to consult with your family doctor, and then with a specialist in the area of psychiatry, neurology, and/or psychology who is knowledgeable in the area of adult ADHD and other conditions.

Living with ADHD is a daily battle which renews itself every morning, but equipped with the proper education, awareness, and personalized treatment plan, you can face the new day feeling prepared and uplifted. This book contains information which aims to alleviate some of the difficulties you face by preparing you for the obstacles in your everyday life: understanding the source of the impairment, developing coping mechanisms and obtaining practical tools for your lifestyle, and raising consciousness of the various treatment options for your condition.

If you have any questions, any comments, or a story to tell about your life with ADHD, please do not hesitate to go to the first author's website and send her an e-mail: www.verajoffe.com

Sincerely,

Vera Joffe, Ph.D.
Monica Iachan, B.A.

# References

Adler, L. (2006). Scattered Minds: Hope and Help for Adults with Attention Deficit Hyperactivity Disorder. New York: Penguin Group.

Adler, L., Kessler, R.C., & Spencer, T. (2003). The Adult ADHD Self-Report Scale (ASRS-v1.1) Symptom Checklist. Geneva, Switzerland: World Health Organization.

Barkley, R.A. (2006). Attention-Deficit Hyperactivity Disorder: A Handbook for Diagnosis and Treatment (3rd ed.). New York: Guilford Press.

Barkley, R.A. (1997). ADHD and the Nature of Self-Control. New York: Guilford Press.

Barkley, R.A. (2004). Personal Communication.

Barkley, R.A. (2005, August). Advancing Research on ADHD in Adults. In V. Joffe & R. A. Barkley (Chairs), Recent Research on ADHD in Adults. Symposium conducted at the annual meeting of the American Psychological Association Meeting. Washington, DC.

Barkley, R.A. & Murphy, K.R. (2006). Attention-deficit hyperactivity disorder: A clinical workbook (3rd ed.). New York: Guilford Press.

Barkley, R.A., Murphy, K.R., DuPaul, G.J. & Bush, T. (2002). Driving in young adults with attention deficit hyperactivity disorder: Knowledge, performance, adverse outcomes, and the role of executive functioning. Journal of International Neuropsychological Society, 8, 655-672.

Biederman, J. (2002). Practical Considerations in Stimulant Drug Selection for the Attention-Deficit/Hyperactivity Disorder Patient-Efficacy, Potency, and Titration. Today's Therapeutic Trends 20(4): 311-328.

Biederman, J.; Mick, E.; Faraone, S.V. (2000). Age dependent decline of symptoms of attention deficit hyperactivity disorder: Impact of remission definition and symptom type. American Journal of Psychiatry, 157: 826-818.

Biederman, J.; Wilens, T.; Mick, E.; Spencer, T.; Faraone, S.V. (1999). Pharmachotherapy of attention/hyperactivity disorder reduces the risk for substance abuse disorder. Pediatrics, 104:20.

Brown, T.E. (1996). Brown Attention Deficit Disorder Scales for Adolescents and Adults. San Antonio, TX: Psychological Corporation.

Chronis, A.M.; Raggi, V.L; Jones, H.A.; Clarke, T.L. & Diaz, Y. (2005, August). Maternal ADHD Symptoms and Parenting: Implications for Child Treatment. In V. Joffe & R. Barkley (Chairs) Recent Research on ADHD in Adults. Symposium conducted at the American Psychological Association, Washington, DC.

Chronis, A.M.; Gamble, S.A.; Roberts, J.E. & Pelham, W. (in press) Cognitive-Behavioral Depression Treatment for Mothers of Children with Attention-Deficit/Hyperactivity Disorder. Behavior Therapy.

Cox, D.J.; Merkel, R.I.; Penberthy, J.K.; Kovatche, V.B. & Hankin, C.S. (2004). Impact of methylphenidate delivery profiles on driving performance of adolescents with ADHD: A pilot study. Journal of American Academy of Child and Adolescent Psychiatry, 43, 269-275.

Fischer, M. (2005, August). Hyperactive Children as Adults: Adaptive Outcomes. In V.Joffe & Barkley, R.A. (Chairs). Recent Research on ADHD in Adults. Symposium conducted at the annual meeting of the American Psychological Association Meeting. Washington, DC.

Jensen, P.S. (2004). Making the System Work for Your Child with ADHD. New York: The Guilford Press.

Wilens, T.E. (2004). Impact of ADHD and its treatment on substance abuse in adults. <u>Journal of Clinical Psychiatry</u>; 65, 38-45.

Wilens, T.E.; Biederman, J.; Spencer, T.J. (2002). Attention deficit/hyperactivity disorder across the lifespan. <u>Annual Rev Med</u>, 53: 113-131.

Recommended websites:

www.chadd.org
www.add.org
www.nih.org
www.nimh.org
www.aacap.org
www.apa.org
www.myadhd.com